The Secret of Rhonda Byrne

or

The Law of Attraction

in the Bible

CONTENTS

Preface

"The Secret of Rhonda Byrne" or "The Law of Attraction" is not a new concept. In fact, it isn't a secret at all. The law of attraction was first promulgated by some of the earliest wise men, and it appears again and again throughout the Bible. But very few people have learned or understand it. That's why it's unfamiliar to many and the reason it remains virtually a secret.

If you were to ask one man after another what the secret of success is, you probably wouldn't run into one man who could tell you. Yet, this information is enormously valuable to us, if we really understand and apply it. It's valuable to us not only for our own lives, but for the lives of those around us – our families, employees, associates and friends.

The principles of the Secret - the principles of success, appear again and again throughout the Bible, if you only look carefully...

One Great Law

There is one great Law that governs the Universe. Its manifestations are multiform, but viewed from the Ultimate there is but one Law. We are familiar with some of its manifestations, but are almost totally ignorant of certain others. Still, we are learning a little more every day - the veil is being gradually lifted.

We speak learnedly of the Law of Gravitation, but ignore that equally wonderful manifestation, THE LAW OF ATTRACTION IN THE THOUGHT WORLD. We are familiar with that wonderful manifestation of Law which draws and holds together the atoms of which matter is composed; we recognize the power of the law that attracts bodies to the earth, that holds the circling worlds in their places - but we close our eyes to the mighty law that draws to us the things we desire or fear, that makes or mars our lives.

When we come to see that *Thought is a force* - a manifestation of energy - having a magnet-like power of attraction, we will begin to understand the why and wherefore of many things that have heretofore seemed dark to us. *There is no study that will so well repay the student for his time and trouble as the study of the workings of this mighty law of the world of Thought - the Law of Attraction.*

When we think, we send out vibrations of a fine ethereal substance, which are as real as the vibrations manifesting light, heat, electricity, and magnetism. That these vibrations are not evident to our five senses is no proof that they do not exist. A powerful magnet will send out vibrations and exert a force sufficient to attract to itself a piece of steel weighing a hundred pounds, but we can neither see, taste, smell, hear nor feel the mighty force. Thought vibrations, likewise, cannot be seen, tasted, smelled, heard nor felt in the ordinary way. (Although it is true there are cases of persons peculiarly sensitive to psychic impressions who have perceived powerful thought-waves, and very many of us can testify that we have distinctly felt the thought vibrations of others, both whilst in the presence of the sender and at a distance. Telepathy and its kindred phenomena are not idle dreams).

It is not necessary to demonstrate the fact that thought vibrations exist. The last-named fact has been fully established to the satisfaction of numerous investigators of the subject, and a little reflection will show you that it coincides with your own experiences. We often hear repeated the well-known Mental Science statement, "Thoughts are Things," and we say these words over without consciously realizing the meaning of the statement. If we fully comprehended the truth of the statement and the natural consequences of the truth back of it, we will understand many things that have appeared dark to us, and will be able to use the wonderful power, Thought Force, just as we use any other manifestation of Energy.

When we think, we set into motion vibrations of a very high degree; and when we understand the laws governing the production and transmission of these vibrations, we will be able to use them in our daily life, just as we do the better known forms of energy. That we cannot see, hear, weigh or measure these vibrations is no proof that they do not exist. There exist waves of sound which no human ear can hear, although some of these are undoubtedly registered by the ear of some of the insects, and others are caught by delicate scientific instruments invented by man. Yet there is a great gap between the sounds registered by the most delicate instrument and the limit which man's mind, reasoning by analogy, knows to be the boundary line between sound waves and some other forms of vibration. And there are light waves which the eye of man does not register, some of which may be detected by more delicate instruments, and many more so fine that the instrument has not yet been invented which will detect them, although improvements are being made every year and the unexplored field gradually lessened. As new instruments are invented, new vibrations are registered by them - and yet the vibrations were just as real before the invention of the instrument as afterward.

Supposing that we had no instruments to register magnetism - one might be justified in denying the existence of that mighty force, because it could not be tasted, felt, smelt, heard, seen, weighted or measured. And yet the mighty magnet would still send out waves of force sufficient to draw to it pieces of steel weighing hundreds of pounds. Each form of vibration requires its own form of instrument for registration.

At present the human brain seems to be the only instrument capable of registering thought waves, although occultists say that in this century scientists will invent apparatus sufficiently delicate to catch and register such impressions. And from present indications it looks as if the invention named might be expected at any time. The demand exists and undoubtedly will be soon supplied. But to those who have experimented along the lines of practical telepathy no further proof is required than the results of their own experiments.

We are sending out thoughts of greater or less intensity all the time, and we are reaping the results of such thoughts. Not only do our thought waves influence ourselves and others, but they have a drawing power - they attract to us the thoughts of others, things, circumstances, people, "luck," in accord with the character of the thought uppermost in our minds.

Thoughts of Love will attract to us the Love of others, circumstances and surroundings in accord with the thought, and people who are of like thought. Thoughts of Anger, Hate, Envy, Malice and Jealousy will draw to us the foul brood of kindred thoughts emanating from the minds of others, circumstances in which we will be called upon to manifest these vile thoughts and receive them in turn from others, people who will manifest inharmony, and so on.

Like attracts like in the Thought World - Birds of the same feather flock together, in the Thought World. The man or woman who is filled with Love sees Love on all sides and attracts the Love of others. The man with Hate in his heart gets all the Hate he can stand. The man who thinks Fight generally runs up against all the Fight he wants before he gets through. And so it goes, each gets what he calls for over the wireless telegraphy of the Mind. The man who rises in the morning feeling "grumpy" usually manages to have the whole family in the same mood before the breakfast is over. The "nagging" woman generally finds enough to gratify her "nagging" propensity during the day.

This matter of Thought Attraction is a serious one. When you stop to think of it you will see that a man really makes his own surroundings, although he blames others for it. I have known people who understood this law to hold a positive, calm thought and be absolutely unaffected by the inharmony surrounding them. They were like the vessel from which the oil had been poured on the troubled waters - they rested safely and calmly whilst the tempest raged around them.

One is not at the mercy of the fitful storms of Thought after he has learned the workings of the Law. We have passed through the age of physical force on to the age of intellectual supremacy, and are now entering a new and almost unknown field, that of psychic or thought power. This field has its established laws and we should acquaint ourselves with them or we will be crowded to the wall as are the ignorant on the planes of effort.

Believe

Blessed is the man who trusts in the LORD

- Jeremiah 17:7

All religions of the world represent forms of belief, and these beliefs are explained in many ways. The law of life is belief.

Realize that the Bible is not talking about belief in some ritual, ceremony, form, institution, man, or formula. Belief is a thought in your mind. The belief of your mind is simply the thought of your mind, which causes the power of your subconscious mind to be manifest in all phases of your life according to your thinking habits. All your experiences, all your actions, and all the events and circumstances of your life are but reflections and reactions to your own thoughts.

15

The prime condition of all success and achivement is faith. Over and over again you read in the Bible, "According to your faith is it done unto you". If you plant certain types of seeds in the ground, you have faith they will grow after their kind. This is the way of seeds, and trusting the laws of growth and agriculture, you know that the seeds will come forth after their kind. Faith as mentioned in the Bible is a way of thinking, an attitude of mind, an inner certitude, knowing that the idea you fully accept in your conscious mind will be embodied in your subconscious mind and made manifest.

Every living thing has faith in something or somebody. It is the quality of the creative energy in the faith thought which gives it vitality. Even intense fear is alive with faith. You fear sickness because you believe it possible for you to contract it. You fear poverty and loneliness because you believe them possible for you.

"For the thing which I did fear is come upon me, and that which I was afraid of hath overtaken me."

- Job 3:25

Your subconscious mind accepts what is impressed upon it or what you consciously believe. Your subconscious mind is like the soil, which accepts any kind of seed, good or bad, without arguing with you controversially. Your thoughts might be likened unto seeds. Negative, destructive thoughts continue to work negatively in your subconscious mind, and in due time will come forth into outer experience which corresponds with them.

Remember, your subconscious mind does not engage in proving whether your thoughts are good or bad, true or false, but it responds according to the nature of your thoughts or suggestions. For example, if you consciously assume something as true, even though it may be false, your subconscious mind will accept it as true and proceed to bring about results, which must necessarily follow, because you consciously assumed it to be true.

Dr. Norman Vincent Peel said this:

"This is one of the greatest laws in the universe. Fervently do I wish I had discovered it as a very young man. It dawned upon me much later in life, and I found it to be one of the greatest, if not my greatest discovery outside of my relationship to God. And the great law briefly and simply stated is that if you think in negative terms, you get negative results. If you think in positive terms, you will achieve positive results."

That is the simple fact at the basis of an astonishing law of prosperity and success. In three words: "Believe, and succeed."

Your right to be rich

The very first chapter of the Bible describes the rich universe created for man. The last book of the Bible symbolically describes heaven in rich terms. Most of the great men of the Bible were either born prosperous, became prosperous or had access to riches whenever the need arose - among them were Abraham, Jacob, Joseph, Moses, David, Solomon, Isaiah, Jeremiah, Nehemiah, Elijah and Elisha. Hence, contrary to popular belief, the Bible clearly shows that you have not been pleasing God by settling for lack and limitation in your life, any more than you have been pleasing yourself

When you realize that God wants you to be prosperous and that God, as the Creator of this rich universe, is indeed the Source of your prosperity, you are not worshipping riches. You are not making prosperity a false god. You are simply claiming your prosperous heritage from the Source of all your blessings.

God pointed out the right spiritual attitude toward prosperity when He told Moses to remind the Children of Israel: *But thou shalt remember the Lord thy God, for it is He that giveth thee power to get wealth.* (Deut. 8:18) The word "wealth" means grand living, and that is what a prosperous thinker should be working toward and should be expecting as his spiritual right.

The object of all life is development; and everything that lives has an inalienable right to all the development it is capable of attaining. Man's right to life means his right to have the free and unrestricted use of all the things which may be necessary to his fullest mental, spiritual, and physical unfoldment. Society is so organized that man must have money in order to become the possessor of things; therefore, the basis of all advancement for man must be the science of getting rich.

Whatever may be said in praise of poverty, the fact remains that it is not possible to live a really complete or successful life unless one is rich. There is nothing wrong in wanting to get rich. 'Desire' is possibility seeking expression, or function seeking performance. The desire for riches is really the desire for a richer, fuller, and more abundant life; and that desire is praiseworthy.

Man cannot live fully in body without good food, comfortable clothing, warm shelter, and without freedom from excessive toil. Rest and recreation are also necessary to his physical life. He cannot live fully in mind without books and time to study them, without opportunity for travel and observation, or without intellectual companionship. To live fully in mind he must have intellectual recreations, and must surround himself with all the objects of art and beauty he is capable of using and appreciating. To live fully in soul, man must have love; and love is denied expression by poverty.

A man's highest happiness is found in the bestowal of benefits on those he loves; love finds its most natural and spontaneous expression in giving. The man who has nothing to give cannot fill his place as a husband or father, as a citizen, or as a man. It is in the use of material things that a man finds full life for his body, develops his mind, and unfolds his soul. It is therefore of supreme importance to him that he should be rich.

Prayer

Ask and it shall be given you

*I am the LORD your God,
who brought you up out of Egypt.
Open wide your mouth and I will
fill it.*

- Psalms 81

This passage refers to God urging us to ask Him for all our needs. By asking God for everything we need, we demostrate our faith in God's power and generosity, which is unlimited.

God is unique. He created us, takes care of us, and wishes to continue to guide us to achieve our utmost.

So Ask!

He will call upon me, and I will
answer him;
I will be with him in trouble,
I will deliver him and honor him.

With long life will I satisfy him
and show him my salvation."

- Psalms 91

In these modem times you hear much about the power of prayer. Prayer is often described as the mightiest force in the universe. You frequently hear such phrases as "prayer changes things" or "the family who prays together stays together." Mail that comes to you may be stamped "pray for peace" or "spiritual action is constructive - the U.N. needs your prayers." Everywhere the power of prayer is being written about, talked about, and used as never before. Someone succinctly described the power of prayer in this manner: "Prayer is profoundly simple and simply profound!"

Recently the vice-president of a large real estate firm talked at length about the power of prayer. He declared, "This is a more spiritual world than many folks realize. People often wear a mask, hesitating to speak of their belief in prayer or of their own answered prayers." He then related how, during a recent period of ill health, his supposedly "hard-boiled business friends" quietly visited him in the hospital and later at home, to talk with him about the power of prayer for restoring his health. Even after he returned to work, several business friends spent their entire lunch periods with him, relating numerous answered prayers in their own life experiences.

Prayer Is Natural to Man

Prayer has been described as man's steady effort to know God. Quite contrary to what most people think, prayer is natural to man, rather than a strange, mysterious practice. Men have always prayed and always will. In his primitive understanding, primitive man prayed to the sun and stars, to the fire and water, to animals and plants, to images and myths, but primitive man certainly prayed.

Later, as the intellect of man evolved, his ideas advanced as he conceived of God as a personal deity who had human sentiments and emotions, just as did primitive man. All men in all ages have prayed in one way or another. At long last, mankind is coming out of a primitive and purely intellectual approach to God into true spiritual understanding. Our methods of prayer are now changing, expanding, and improving. Mankind is finally realizing that God is not a hostile Being with a split personality of good and evil, but that God is a God of love, the unchanging principle of supreme good which pervades the ordered universe. It is easy to pray to and commune with this kind of God!

Pray for Results

Even though various prosperity laws are discussed in this book, the power of prayer cannot be over-emphasized for permanent, satisfying prosperity. The person who prays daily is certain to succeed, because he is attuning himself to the richest, most successful force in the universe.

The Bible promises make it plain that there's nothing wrong with praying for things. Many people have not employed the power of prayer because they have the erroneous idea that it is wrong to pray for things.

It is right and just that you should pray for things if you need them, because you are living in a rich universe that desires to fulfill all your needs. Among Biblical figures who prayed for definite things were Abraham, Daniel, David, Elijah, Ezekiel, Habakkuk, Hannah, Jehoshaphat, Jeremiah, Jonah, Joshua, Moses, Nehemiah, Samson, and Solomon.

Tennyson poetically expressed the power of praying for things in his line: "More things are wrought by prayer than this world dreams".

Emmet Fox once described the power of praying for things as follows:

"Prayer does change things. Prayer does make things to happen quite otherwise than they would have happened had the prayer not been made. It makes no difference at all what sort of difficulty you may be in. It does not matter what the causes may have been that led up to it. Enough prayer will get you out of your difficulty, if only you will be persistent enough in your appeal to God." (*The Sermon on the Mount,* Harper & Brothers, New York, p. 11).

Perhaps you have heard the well-worn phrase, "Pray about it and everything will be all right." Here are four basic ways of praying so that everything will be all right:

1.General Prayer

General prayer is praying to God as a loving, understanding Father in your own private way. It can be on your knees, or in any comfortable position. It can be expressed in spoken words or in silent communion. It can be with a prayer book before you, or it can be by browsing through your Bible, dwelling upon favorite passages, or paraphrasing them to meet your need.

A good way to begin using a general prayer is to take the Lord's Prayer and to consider each line of it silently and verbally. The ancients believed that the Lord's Prayer was all-powerful; they often declared it over and over from twelve to fifteen times without stopping. The number fifteen was believed to have the power to dissolve affliction and adversity.

Sometimes one form of general prayer will aid you, and at other times some other form will meet your need. In this age when we're hearing a great deal about affirmative prayer, which is often described as "scientific prayer," as well as about meditation and silent prayer, it is good to remember that good, old-fashioned earnest prayer, used in a general way, has not gone out of style and still contains great spiritual power.

Prayer Heals

A businessman once related how general prayer met a need in his family. His little son had been ill for several weeks with a serious cough. Medical attention had been of no avail and the cough persisted. One night in desperation this man took his pajama-clad son into the den of his home and sank into the nearest chair. He then offered a short, simple general prayer of thanks that his son was healed of the cough and infection. In any event, the child coughed only twice after that, and completely recovered! That is the power of general prayer.

General Prayer and the Law of Command

The secret of the law of command is this: A positive assertion of the good you wish to experience is often all that is needed to turn the tide of events to produce good for you swiftly and easily. It's amazing how fast doors open to us when we dare to take control of a situation and command our high expectations to manifest themselves. But there's nothing new about the law of command. In Genesis we are told that God created the earth by commanding, *Let there be . . . and there was.*

Actually the law of command is one of the easiest to use. After having made lists of your desires and after having mentally imaged them as fulfilled, it is then time to release the substance of them into words of decree and command which can move the ethers into action.

What you decree you get, as the Bible promises, for *Thou shalt decree a thing and it shall be established unto thee and light shall shine upon thy ways.* (Job 22:28)

If you feel that perhaps your prayer experience has not been satisfying or powerful, and that nothing much happened as a result of your prayers, perhaps it is because you would like to develop more specific types of prayer than general prayer.

2. Prayers of Denial

The second type of prayer is one little known or understood. It is the prayer of denial.

Many people cringe at the word "denial," believing that its only meaning is "to take away or withhold." But the word "deny" also means: "to dissolve, to erase or be free from, to refuse to accept as true or right that which is reported to be true." Prayers of denial are for the latter purpose - to refuse to accept as necessary, true, lasting, or right anything that is not satisfying or good.

Prayers of denial are your "no" prayers. They help you to reject things as they are, and to dissolve your negative thoughts about them, and make way for something better. Prayers of denial help you to erase, to be free from less than the best in your life. Prayers of denial are expressed in those attitudes that think, "I will not put up with or tolerate this experience as necessary, lasting or right. I refuse to accept things as they are. I am God's child and I will accept nothing but His complete goodness for me."

It is good to follow up thoughts of what you don't want with what you do want; after claiming "no, I will not accept this," you should add, "yes, I will accept this or something better."

Long ago, the Egyptians followed the command to take away all iniquity through the power of denial. The Egyptians used the sign of the cross to indicate a crossing out or blotting out of evil, a form of denial which still is used by some churches.

How to Dissolve Fear, Worry, Tension

Prayers of denial dissolve fear, worry, sorrow, sickness, tension, and other negative emotions. "No" prayers seem to neutralize the effects of negation.

In speaking of this second type of prayer, as well as the third type of prayer - denial and affirmation - note that they are as much attitudes of mind as formal methods of prayer. You can use them silently or verbally wherever you are, either as formal prayers, or informally as attitudes of mind.

Any secretary knows the feeling when she is hurriedly called in for dictation, and informed that she must produce quick results. It can be confusing and upsetting unless one knows how to use "no" attitudes of mind. For example, a legal secretary was informed that a long legal contract that had been dictated to her had to be transcribed immediately (if not sooner!) for one of the boss's prominent clients. It seemed an impossible task, and so she began thinking over and over: **There is no need to rush. Divine Order is now established and**

maintained in this situation. Within a few minutes, this client changed his mind about the urgency of this matter, and informed the boss he would return the next day to sign the papers. This allowed time to prepare them properly.

So many people get the erroneous idea that somebody else can keep their good from them, and so they unhappily go through life believing it. Prayers of denial can dissolve such falsity. When you catch yourself thinking in such a limited vein, change the thought and declare, **Nothing can oppose my good.** As you do, you will find that, where people and affairs seemed to work against you, everything will shift and begin working for you.

One of the greatest problems of mankind is how to overcome and dissolve fear. When you can overcome your fear of any problem, you have gained control of it; it no longer controls you; and you are well on the way to solving it. A powerful prayer to deny fear is: **Perfect love casts out fear.**

Say "No" to Unhappiness

A war bride came to this country with her American husband. For a few years they seemed happy, but then the old memories of her war experiences began welling up in her mind. She became very unhappy, depressed, and confused. Finally, her husband had her confined to a mental hospital. Later, he divorced her and remarried.

In the midst of all this unhappiness, far from her homeland, among strangers, this woman learned of the "no" attitude of mind. She had only one friend outside of the hospital, to whom she began to write, "I am not going to remain in my present condition. I know I can be helped. I know I am going to get well." Gradually, she began to improve. Soon she was released from the hospital and went to work in another hospital. When she did, she declared to her friend, "You see, I told you I had what it takes." She was soon happily married to a doctor whom she met at her new job.

If people only knew how to say "no" to unhappy experiences, rather than to bow down to them!

To declare, **There is nothing for me to fear. God's spirit of good is at work and Divine Results are coming forth** is to dissolve fear, worry, tension, anxiety. To declare (as the scientists know), **There is no absence of life, substance or intelligence anywhere, so there is no absence of life**, substance or intelligence in this situation or in my life** dissolves uncertainty, confusion and many times dissipates psychomatic sickness or financial lack.

Immunize Yourself Against Negation

The denial attitude of mind does not invite trouble by discussing it. The denial attitude of mind mentally says "no" to talk of others which emphasizes less than the best, or that gives attention to what you don't want to experience. Instead of multiplying problems by discussing them loud and long; instead of fretting about world conditions or the problems of others, do whatever you constructively can to make them right. Use the "No, I will not accept this as lasting, permanent, or necessary" attitude toward all.

When people try to upset or bother you with a lot of negative talk, mentally say, "No, no, no, I do not wish to hear this. I do not accept this as true or necessary." Soon they will either switch to more constructive topics, or leave!

In like manner, instead of thinking that you have to "put up with" dissatisfaction in your life as a permanent arrangement, use your "no" power by declaring often: **No, I do not have to accept this situation. God in his almighty goodness is dissolving and removing all negation from my world. No situation dismays me, for God the Spirit of Good is with me, upholding and sustaining me and making all things right.**

For financial affairs, here is a prayer of denial: **Regardless of taxes, high cost of living or the high rate of unemployment, my financial income can and does increase richly now through the direct action of God.**

When you dare to use your "no" power of mind on a loud, boisterous, unhappy situation, you then gain mental and emotional control of it, rather than letting it control you. You are then shown what outer, positive steps to take to meet it victoriously.

3. Prayers of Affirmation

The third type of prayer affirmations should be used with denials. When you use denials, you erase, dissolve, liquidate. You then wish to make firm new good, which is done through affirmative prayers.

A traveling salesman once told how he did this. He had been heavily in debt and had attempted to get a loan from a bank to pay off his debts. Because he lacked adequate security, he had not been able to obtain a loan. In desperation, he decided to say "no" to his indebtedness and "yes" to prosperity. So he constantly affirmed: **God prospers me now.** Within a few days after he began declaring this, he made the largest sale he had ever made, after which he was able to pay off all his debts, with ample supply left over.

4. Prayers of Meditation and Silence

The fourth type of prayer is the prayer of meditation and silence. It is often in meditation and silent, contemplative prayer that you feel the presence of God's goodness most strongly. In this type of prayer, you take a few meaningful words and think about them and feed upon them silently. As you think about them and contemplate them, they grow in your mind as expanded ideas that move you to right action, or perhaps as peaceful assurance that all is well and no action is needed. If nothing seems to happen in meditation, you have nevertheless made the mind receptive to God's good and at the right time, ideas and opportunities will be revealed as a result of your spiritual exercise in meditation.

Perhaps you are thinking, "This is all pretty good spiritual theory, but how do I know that meditation and silent prayer will produce tangible, satisfying results in my work-a-day world?" Moses and other Biblical leaders proved the practical, result-getting power of silent meditation.

Perhaps you are thinking, "But I'm no Moses, and I frankly am not sure how to practice meditation and silent prayer." The truth is, that you meditate whether you've been aware of it or not. Everyone does. The word "meditate" means: "To think about, contemplate, to consider deeply and continuously."

How to Meditate

Whatever you think about constantly is the subject of your meditation. In silent prayer it is good to meditate upon the divine solution of any problem. You can begin by just taking the term "divine solution" and letting the thought grow in your mind. You can take some spiritual word or phrase, think about it, and let it unfold to you, or you can simply clear your mind, close your eyes, turn your attention within your own being, and think of "God", "love", "God is love", "peace", or any such idea that gives you a feeling of oneness with good in a relaxed way.

Silent meditation can be used to get guidance or the feeling of renewal, uplift, encouragement and new energy. Someone has said that: "Prayer feeds." Many can affirm that meditation feeds them emotionally with a sense of harmony, uplift and peace; that meditation feeds them intellectually with new ideas, or flashes into their mind something they need to know about a current situation; and that meditation feeds them physically with a sense of body renewal, new energy, and well-being, dissolving fatigue and tension.

Meditation Solves Problems

It is not necessary to be highly developed spiritually to use the power of silent meditation effectively.

Some of the most thrilling results are realized when we take up a problem, sit alone and meditate as follows: **The Divine Solution is the sublime solution. I accept and claim the Divine Solution in this situation now.** Gently let your mind expand on that thought. The "fear energy" spent in worry and battling with the problem will then be transmuted into "faith energy," giving you the right ideas and the right answers. Always, when you have a problem, if you will go into silent meditation and contemplate the solution from a divine standpoint, you will be shown what to do.

An engineering executive once told how he uses this method: When his men run into difficulty on an engineering project, he privately takes the problem, goes into his study, silently meditates upon it from a divine standpoint, and inevitably receives the solution. One of his junior executives once asked him how he always managed to have right answers just when they were needed most. When he explained his simple method, the junior executive skeptically declared, "You mean you just meditate upon the solution, rather than fight the problem?" The business world is full of harried, tense people who became that way through trying to solve their problems in external ways, rather than through the "inner short-cut."

Everyone should take time daily for quiet and meditation. In daily meditation lies your secret of power. It is the only way in which you will ever gain definite knowledge, newness of experience, steadiness of purpose, or power to meet the unknown in daily living victoriously. As you begin to daily practice meditating, you will discover that some of your activities and demands are no longer necessary, and that it is best to let them go, rather than neglect your quiet time of meditation and aloneness with yourself and your creator.

When you withdraw from the world for meditation, it is best not to think of your failures. Instead, calm yourself and center your attention on God and his almighty goodness. If possible, let all the little annoying cares go for a while, and turn your thoughts to some of the simple words of the Psalmist. Hold in mind some thoughts that help you, be it ever so simple: "I and the Father are one", "Thy will be done in me", "I love you, God", "Thank you, Father", "I am in thy presence, Lord", "This is the day that the Lord hath made, I will rejoice and be glad in it", "Peace, be still".

Until you have practiced the presence of God in the simple way, you can have no idea how it quiets all physical nervousness, all fear, all oversensitivness, all the little raspings of everyday life. A time of calm, quiet waiting, alone with God, is one of restfulness and renewal. This is the "secret place of the most High" of which the Psalmist speaks.

Of the four types of prayer: general, denial, affirmative, or meditative, use whatever type seems appropriate to you at the moment, or perhaps blend the several types. But pray often! It can be the secret of peace, power and plenty.

Hope to God;
Be strong and fortify yourself,
and Hope to God.

- Psalms 27

If a person sees that his prayers were not answered, let him pray again. As it says:

Hope to God; Be strong and fortify yourself, and Hope to God. (Again)

God's "no" may be merely a "you're not ready for it yet!" As related in the Bible, Isaac and Rebecca prayed for children for 20 years:

***"Isaac prayed to the LORD on
behalf of his wife, because she was
barren. The LORD answered his
prayer, and his wife Rebekah
became pregnant"***
- Genesis 25:21

Visualization - The Imaging Law

Throughout the ages man has believed in an invisible power, through which and by which all things have been created and are continually being re-created. We may personalize this power and call it God, or we may think of it as the essence or spirit which permeates all things, but in either case the effect is the same.

The Bible says we are made "in the image of God". This means we, like God, are creators!

So far as the individual is concerned, the objective - the physical, the visible - is the personal, that which can be cognized by the senses. It consists of body, brain and nerves. The subjective is the spiritual, the invisible, the impersonal.

The personal is conscious because it is a personal entity. The impersonal, being the same in kind and quality as all other Beings, is not conscious of itself and has therefore been termed the subconscious. The personal, or conscious, has the power of will and choice, and can therefore exercise discrimination in the selection of methods whereby to bring about the solution of difficulties. The impersonal, or spiritual, being a part or one with the Source and Origin of all power, can necessarily exercise no such choice, but, on the contrary, it has Infinite resources at its command. It can and does bring about results by methods concerning which the human or individual mind can have no possible conception.

You will therefore see that it is your privilege to depend upon the human will with all its limitations and misconceptions, OR you may utilize the potentialities of Infinity by making use of the subconscious mind. Here, then, is the scientific explanation of the wonderful power that has been put within your control, if you but understand, appreciate and recognize it.

Visualization is the process of making mental images, and the image is the mold or model which will serve as a pattern from which your future will emerge. Hold your desired image firmly in mind and you will gradually and constantly bring the thing nearer to you. Hence, you can be what you will to be.

To use the Law of Imaging, or visualization, make your mental image clear and beautiful. Do not be afraid; make it grand. Remember that no limitation can be placed upon you by anyone but yourself. You are not limited as to cost or material. Draw on the Infinite for your supply and construct it in your imagination; it will have to be there before it will ever appear anywhere else.

The first step is idealization. It is likewise the most important step, because it is the plan on which you are going to build. It must be solid; it must be permanent. The architect, when he plans a 30-story building, has every line and detail pictured in advance. The engineer, when he spans a chasm, first ascertains the strength requirements of a million separate parts.

They see the end before a single step is taken; so you are to picture in your mind what you want. You are sowing the seed, but before sowing any seed you want to know what the harvest is to be. This is Idealization. If you are not sure, return to image daily until the picture becomes plain; it will gradually unfold. First the general plan will be dim, but it will take shape, the outline will take form, then the details, and you will gradually develop the power by which you will be enabled to formulate plans which will eventually materialize in the objective world. You will come to know what the future holds for you.

Then comes the process of visualization. You must see the picture more and more complete, see the detail, and as the details begin to unfold, the ways and means for bringing it into manifestation will develop. One thing will lead to another. Thought will lead to action, action will develop methods, methods will develop friends, and friends will bring about circumstances, and, finally, the third step, or Materialization, will have been accomplished.

We all recognize the Universe must have been thought into shape before it ever could have become a material fact. And if we are willing to follow along the lines of the Great Architect of the Universe, we shall find our thoughts taking form, just as the universe took concrete form. It is the same mind operating through the individual. There is no difference in kind or quality; the only difference is one of degree.

The architect visualizes his building; he sees it as he wishes it to be. His thought becomes a plastic mold from which the building will eventually emerge, a high one or a low one, a beautiful one or a plain one. His vision takes form on paper and eventually the necessary material is utilized and the building stands complete.

The inventor visualizes his idea in exactly the same manner. For instance, Nikola Tesla, he with the giant intellect, one of the greatest inventors of all ages, the man who has brought forth the most amazing realities, always visualizes his inventions before attempting to work them out. He did not rush to embody them in form and then spend his time in correcting defects. Having first built up the idea in his imagination, he held it there as a mental picture, to be reconstructed and improved by his thought. "In this way," he writes in the *Electrical Experimenter*, "I am enabled to rapidly develop and perfect a conception without touching anything. When I have gone so far as to embody in the invention every possible improvement I can think of, and see no fault anywhere, I put into concrete the product of my brain. Invariably my device works as I conceived it should; in twenty years there has not been a single exception."

If you can conscientiously follow these directions, you will develop Faith, the kind of Faith that is the "Substance of things hoped for, the evidence of things not seen". You will develop confidence, the kind of confidence that leads to endurance and courage. You will develop the power of concentration which will enable you to exclude all thoughts except the ones which are associated with your purpose.

The law is that thought will manifest in form. Clearness and accuracy are obtained only by repeatedly having the image in mind, and in proportion to the clearness and accuracy of the image will the outward manifestation be.

You must build it firmly and securely in your mental world, the world within, before it can take form in the world without, and you can build nothing of value, even in the mental world unless you have the proper material. When you have the material you can build anything you wish, but make sure of your material. This material will be brought out by millions of silent mental workers and fashioned into the form of the image which you have in mind.

Think of it! You have over five million of these mental workers, ready and in active use; brain cells they are called. Besides this, there is another reserve force of at least an equal number, ready to be called into action at the slightest need. Your power to think, then, is almost unlimited, and this means that your power to create the kind of material which is necessary to build for yourself any kind of environment which you desire is practically unlimited.

In addition to these millions of mental workers, you have billions of mental workers in the body, every one of which is endowed with sufficient intelligence to understand and act upon any message or suggestion given. These cells are all busy creating and recreating the body, but in addition to this, they are endowed with psychic activity whereby they can attract to themselves the substance necessary for perfect development.

They do this by the same law and in the same manner that every form of life attracts to itself the necessary material for growth. The oak, the rose, the lily, all require certain material for their most perfect expression and they secure it by silent demand, by **the Law of Attraction** - the most certain way for you to secure what you require for your most complete development.

Make the Mental Image. Make it clear, distinct, perfect; hold it firmly. The ways and means will develop, supply will follow the demand, and you will be led to do the right thing at the right time and in the right way. Earnest Desire will bring about Confident Expectation, and this in turn must be reinforced by Firm Demand. These three cannot fail to bring about Attainment, because the Earnest Desire is the feeling, the Confident Expectation is the thought, and the Firm Demand is the will, and as we have seen, feeling gives vitality to thought and the will holds it steadily until the law of Growth brings it into manifestation.

Is it not wonderful that man has such tremendous power within himself, such transcendental faculties concerning which he had no conception? Is it not strange that we have always been taught to look for strength and power "without?" We have been taught to look everywhere but "within" and whenever this power manifested in our lives we were told that it was something supernatural.

There are many who have come to an understanding of this wonderful power, and who make serious and conscientious efforts to realize health, power and other conditions, and seem to fail. They do not seem able to bring the Law into operation. The difficulty in nearly every case is that they are dealing with externals. They want money, power, health and abundance, but they fail to realize that these are effects and can come only when the cause is found.

Those who will give no attention to the world without will seek only to ascertain the truth, will look only for wisdom, will find that this wisdom will unfold and disclose the source of all power, that it will manifest in thought and purpose which will create the external conditions desired. This truth will find expression in noble purpose and courageous action.

Create ideals only. Give no thought to external conditions. Make the world within beautiful and opulent, and the world without will express and manifest the conditions which you have within. You will come into a realization of your power to create ideals and these ideals will be projected into the world of effect.

For instance, a man is in debt. He will be continually thinking about the debt, concentrating on it, and as thoughts are causes the result is that he not only fastens the debt closer to him, but he actually creates more debt. He is putting the great law of Attraction into operation with the usual and inevitable result - Loss leads to greater "Loss."

What, then, is the correct principle? Concentrate on the things you want, not on the things you do not want. Think of abundance; idealize the methods and plans for putting the Law of Abundance into operation. Visualize the condition which the Law of Abundance creates; this will result in manifestation.

If the law operates perfectly to bring about poverty, lack and every form of limitation for those who are continually entertaining thoughts of lack and fear, it will operate with the same certainty to bring about conditions of abundance and opulence for those who entertain thoughts of courage and power.

This is a difficult problem for many. We are too anxious; we manifest anxiety, fear, distress; we want to do something; we want to help; we are like a child who has just planted a seed and every fifteen minutes goes and stirs up the earth to see if it is growing. Of course, under such circumstances, the seed will never germinate, and yet this is exactly what many of us do in the mental world.

We must plant the seed and leave it undisturbed. This does not mean that we are to sit down and do nothing, by no means; we will do more and better work then we have ever done before, new channels will constantly be provided, new doors will open. All that is necessary is to have an open mind, be ready to act when the time comes.

Thought force is the most powerful means of obtaining knowledge, and if concentrated on any subject will solve the problem. Nothing is beyond the power of human comprehension, but in order to harness thought force and make it do your bidding, work is required.

Remember that thought is the fire that creates the steam that turns the wheel of fortune, upon which your experiences depend.

Ask yourself a few questions and then reverently await the response. Do you not now and then feel the self with you? Do you assert this self or do you follow the majority? Remember that majorities are always led; they never lead. It was the majority that fought, tooth and nail, against the steam engine, the power loom and every other advance or improvement ever suggested.

In the Book of Genesis, we are told how Joseph proved the power of the imagination for success and prosperity. From him we learn what to do and what not to do with our imagination. In Joseph's dreams at the age of 17, he had dominion over the situations about which he dreamed. In one dream his brothers' sheaves were bowing down to Joseph's sheaf. In another dream, the sun, moon and stars were honoring Joseph. These dreams were symbolic of the dominion Joseph was to have later as prime minister of Egypt.

Joseph dreamed of dominion, and so must you. Joseph dreamed of dominion when he seemed to have none, and so must you. Success is created mentally first. But Joseph made the mistake of telling his dreams to his jealous brothers, who resented his claims of dominion, so they sold him for 20 pieces of silver, to some Ishmaelite merchants on their way to Egypt. Unlike Joseph, you should not tell your dreams and mental images of greater good to others, who will only try to tear down your pictures of grandeur with their doubt and unbelief.

After Joseph was sold into Egyptian slavery, he apparently continued to image better than the best he was then experiencing. He proved that vision is victory; he also proved that the victim can become the victor! When he arrived in Egypt, he had to meet a number of unjust experiences before the tide turned for him. Only after years in prison and many tribulations did Joseph become prime minister of all Egypt, second in command of the most powerful empire of that age.

Persist in Picturing Success

Sometimes the imaging power of the mind produces immediate results for you. But if (like Joseph) it takes longer, you can be assured that the results will be even bigger when they do come, provided you do not get discouraged and give up. The longer it takes your mental images to produce results, the bigger they will be, if you hold on to them.

The Power of Words

Throughout the Bible, many references are made to words and their creative power for good. The creation story began with the spoken affirmation, *Let there be . . . and there was.* (Gen. 1) The writer of Proverbs might have been speaking of the power of words for healing when he wrote, *Death and life are in the power of the tongue, and they that love it shall eat the fruit thereof.* (Prov. 18:21)

Power goes into our words according to the feeling and faith behind them. When we realize the power that moves the world is moving on our behalf and is backing up our word, our confidence and assurance grow. You do not try and add power to power; therefore, there must be no mental striving, coercion, force, or mental wrestling.

A young girl used the *decree method* of words on a young man who was constantly phoning her, pressing her for dates, and meeting her at her place of business; she found it very difficult to get rid of him. She decreed as follows: "I release.........unto God. He is in his true place at all times. I am free, and he is free. I now decree that my words go forth into infinite mind and it brings it to pass. It is so." She said he vanished and she has never seen him since, adding, "It was as though the ground swallowed him up."

Thou shalt decree a thing, and it shall be established unto thee: and the light shall shine upon thy ways.

- Job 22:28

As a man thinketh

The way one looks at the world is the kind of world he shall have. This principle is derived from Proverbs 4:23:

"Guard your mind more than everything else, for from it come all the results of life!"

Have you ever thought about food and found yourself hungry?

Think about a tragic situation, and soon you'll feel sad, maybe ever begin to cry.

The thought itself motivates your body to participate.

One who decides to gain more happiness and peace of mind, and embarks on the career of seeking the good in all things and all people, will find he is looking for. Just thinking about it makes it happen.

The aphorism, "As a man thinketh in his heart so is he," not only embraces the whole of a man's being, but is so comprehensive as to reach out to every condition and circumstance of his life. A man is literally what he thinks, his character being the complete sum of all his thoughts.

As the plant springs from and could not be without the seed, so every act of man springs from the hidden seeds of thought, and could not have appeared without them. This applies equally to those acts called "spontaneous" and "unpremeditated" as to those that are deliberately executed.

Action is the blossom of thought, and joy and suffering are its fruit; thus does a man garner in the sweet and bitter fruitage of his own husbandry.

Man is a growth by law, and not a creation by artifice, and cause and effect are as absolute and undeviating in the hidden realm of thought as in the world of visible and material things. A noble and God-like character is not a thing of favor or chance, but is the natural result of continued effort in right thinking, the effect of long-cherished association with God-like thoughts. An ignoble and bestial character, by the same process, is the result of the continued harboring of groveling thoughts.

Man is made or unmade by himself. In the armory of thought he forges the weapons by which he destroys himself. He also fashions the tools with which he builds for himself heavenly mansions of joy and strength and peace. By the right choice and true application of thought, man ascends to the divine perfection. By the abuse and wrong application of thought he descends below the level of the beast. Between these two extremes are all the grades of character, and man is their maker and master.

"And we seemed like grasshoppers in our own eyes, and we looked the same (like grasshoppers) in their eyes."

- Numbers 13:33

When you view yourself as inferior, others will view you in the same manner. You will project your image and your thoughts to others.

Each one of us constantly uses the law of radiation and attraction whether we are aware of it or not. But if you wish to enjoy more prosperity and success in life, you have to consciously, boldly and deliberately take hold of your thoughts and feelings and redirect them toward prosperity and success. It is up to you to dare to choose and radiate outward through your thinking what you really wish to experience in life, rather than to get bogged down in unpleasant or failure experiences of the moment. These conditions can change as quickly as you can change your thinking about them.

Of all the beautiful truths pertaining to the soul which have been restored and brought to light in this age, none is more gladdening or fruitful of divine promise and confidence than this - that man is the master of thought, the molder of character, and the maker and shaper of condition, environment, and destiny.

As a being of power, intelligence, and love, and the lord of his own thoughts, man holds key to every situation, and contains within himself that transforming and regenerative agency by which he may make himself what he wills.

Man is always the master, even in his weakest and most abandoned state. But in his weakness and degradation he is foolish master who misgoverns his "household." When he begins to reflect upon his condition and search diligently for the law upon which his being is established, he then becomes the wise master, directing his energies with intelligence and fashioning his thoughts to fruitful issues. Such is the conscious master, and man can only thus become by discovering within himself the laws of thought. This discovery is totally a matter of application, self-analysis and experience.

Only by much searching and mining are gold and diamonds obtained, and man can find every truth connected with his being, if he will dig deep into the mine of his soul. That he is the maker of his character, the molder of his life, and the builder of his destiny, he may unerringly prove - if he will watch, control, and alter his thoughts, tracing their effects upon himself, upon others and upon his life and circumstances, linking cause and effect by patient practice and investigation. In this direction is the law of absolute that: *"He that seeketh findeth; and to him that knocketh it shall be opened."*

Gratitude

Give thanks to the LORD, for he is good;
his love endures forever.

- Psalms 118

A powerful prayer is one of gratitude. The more we count our blessings, the more blessings come to us. Our thoughts and prayers really do create our experiences!

The whole process of mental adjustment and atonement can be summed up in one word: gratitude.

First, you believe that there is one Intelligent Substance, from which all things proceed; second, you believe that this Substance gives you everything you desire; and third, you relate yourself to it by a feeling of deep and profound gratitude.

Many people who order their lives rightly in all other ways are kept in poverty by their lack of gratitude. Having received one gift from God, they cut the wires which connect them with Him by failing to make acknowledgment. It is easy to understand that the nearer we live to the source of wealth, the more wealth we shall receive; and it is easy also to understand that the soul that is always grateful lives in closer touch with God than the one which never looks to Him in thankful acknowledgment.

The more gratefully we fix our minds on the Supreme when good things come to us, the more good things we will receive, and the more rapidly they will come; and the reason simply is that the mental attitude of gratitude draws the mind into closer touch with the source from which the blessings come. If it is a new thought to you that gratitude brings your whole mind into closer harmony with the creative energies of the universe, consider it well, and you will see that it is true. The good things you already have have come to you along the line of obedience to certain laws. Gratitude will lead your mind out along the ways by which things come; and it will keep you in close harmony with creative thought and prevent you from falling into competitive thought. Gratitude alone can keep you looking toward the All, and prevent you from falling into the error of thinking of the supply as limited.

There is a Law of Gratitude, and it is absolutely necessary that you should observe the law, if you are to get the results you seek. The law of gratitude is the natural principle that action and reaction are always equal, and in opposite directions. The grateful outreaching of your mind in thankful praise to the Supreme is a liberation or expenditure of force; it cannot fail to reach that to which it addressed, and the reaction is an instantaneous movement towards you. "Draw nigh unto God, and He will draw nigh unto you." That is a statement of psychological truth.

And if your gratitude is strong and constant, the reaction in Formless Substance will be strong and continuous; the movement of the things you want will be always toward you. You cannot exercise much power without gratitude; for it is gratitude that keeps you connected with Power. But the value of gratitude does not consist solely in getting you more blessings in the future. Without gratitude you cannot long keep from dissatisfied thought regarding things as they are.

The moment you permit your mind to dwell with dissatisfaction upon things as they are, you begin to lose ground. You fix attention upon the common, the ordinary, the poor, and the squalid and mean; and your mind takes the form of these things. Then you will transmit these forms or mental images to the Formless, and the common, the poor, the squalid, and mean will come to you. To permit your mind to dwell upon the inferior is to become inferior and to surround yourself with inferior things. On the other hand, to fix your attention on the best is to surround yourself with the best, and to become the best.

The Creative Power within us makes us into the image of that to which we give our attention. We are Thinking Substance, and thinking substance always takes the form of that which it thinks about. The grateful mind is constantly fixed upon the best; therefore it tends to become the best; it takes the form or character of the best, and will receive the best.

Also, faith is born of gratitude. The grateful mind continually expects good things, and expectation becomes faith. The reaction of gratitude upon one's own mind produces faith; and every outgoing wave of grateful thanksgiving increases faith. He who has no feeling of gratitude cannot long retain a living faith; and without a living faith you cannot get rich by the creative method.

It is necessary, then, to cultivate the habit of being grateful for every good thing that comes to you; and to give thanks continuously. And because all things have contributed to your advancement, you should include all things in your gratitude. Do not waste time thinking or talking about shortcomings or wrong actions of autocrats and magnates. Their organization of the world has made your opportunity; all you get really comes to you because of them. Do not rage against corrupt politicians; if it were not for politicians we should fall into anarchy, and your opportunity would be greatly lessened.

God has worked a long time and very patiently to bring us up to where we are in industry and government, and He is going right on with His work. There is not the least doubt that He will do away with plutocrats, trust magnates, captains of industry, and politicians as soon as they can be spared; but in the meantime, behold they are all very good. Remember that they are all helping to arrange the lines of transmission along which your riches will come to you, and be grateful to them all. This will bring you into harmonious relations with the good in everything, and the good in everything will move toward you.

How can I repay the LORD for all his goodness to me?

- Psalms 116

Desire

*You open your hand
and satisfy the desires of every
living thing.*

- Psalms 145

In this verse of Psalms, King David is teaching us that God open His hands and satisfies the desires of every living thing.

However, desire is not a hope! It's not a wish! It must be a pulsating desire, which transcends everything else. It needs to be DEFINITE.

And then DESIRE will be translated into reality.

The successful person chooses a definite goal, invests in it all his energy, all his will power, all his effort; everything back of that goal. He is content to start in the most menial work, as long as it provides an opportunity to take even one step toward his cherished goal.

It is told that a great warrior once faced a situation making it necessary for him to make a decision that insured his success on the battlefield. He was about to send his armies against a powerful foe whose men outnumbered his own. He loaded his soldiers into boats, sailed them to the enemy's country, unloaded the soldiers and equipment, and then gave the order to burn the ships that had carried them. Addressing his men before the battle, he said, "You see the boats going up in smoke. That means that we cannot leave these shores alive unless we win! We now have no choice: We win - or we perish!" They won.

Every person who wishes to win in any undertaking must be willing to burn his ships and cut all sources of retreat. Only by so doing can one be sure of maintaining that state of mind known as a BURNING DESIRE TO WIN, essential to success.

The morning after the great Chicago fire, a group of merchants stood on State Street, looking at the smoking remains of what had been their stores. They went into a conference to decide if they would try to rebuild, or leave Chicago and start over in a more promising section of the country. They reached a decision - all except one - to leave Chicago.

The merchant who decided to stay and rebuild pointed a finger at the remains of his store and said, "Gentlemen, on that very spot I will build the world's greatest store, no matter how many times it may burn down."

That was more than hundred years ago. The store was built. It stands there today, a towering monument to the power of that state of mind known as a BURNING DESIRE. The easy thing for Marshal Field to have done would have been exactly what his fellow merchants did. When the going was hard, and the future looked dismal, they pulled up and went where the going seemed easier. Mark well this difference between Marshal Field and the other merchants, because it is the same difference that distinguishes Edwin C. Barnes from thousands of other young men who have worked in the Edison organization. It is the same difference that distinguishes practically all who succeed from those who fail.

Every human being who reaches the age of understanding the purpose of money wishes for it. Wishing will not bring riches. But desiring riches with a state of mind that becomes an obsession, then planning definite ways and means to acquire riches, and backing those plans with persistence which does not recognize failure, will bring riches.

You must get in love with the thing you want, and you must get in love with it in earnest - none of this latter-day flirting, "on-today and off-tomorrow" sort of love, but the good old-fashioned kind, that used to make it impossible for a young man to get to sleep unless he took a walk around his best girl's house, just to be sure it was still there. That's the real kind! And the man or woman in search of success must make of that desired thing his ruling passion - he must keep his mind on the main chance.

Success is jealous - that's why we speak of her as feminine. She demands a man's whole affection, and if he begins flirting with other fair charmers, she soon turns her back upon him. If a man allows his strong interest in the main chance to be sidetracked, he will be the loser.

Mental Force operates best when it is concentrated. You must give to the desired thing your best and most earnest thought. Just as the man who is thoroughly in love will think out plans and schemes whereby he may please the fair one, so will the man who is in love with his work or business give it his best thought, and the result will be that a hundred and one plans will come into his field of consciousness, many of which are very important. The mind works on the subconscious plane, remember, and almost always along the lines of the ruling passion or desire. It will fix up things, and patch together plans and schemes, and when you need them the most it will pop them into your consciousness, and you will feel like hurrahing, just as if you had received some valuable aid from outside.

But if you scatter your thought-force, the subconscious mind will not know just how to please you, and the result is that you are apt to be put off from this source of aid and assistance. Beside this, you will miss the powerful result of concentrated thought in the conscious working out of the details of your plans. And then again the man whose mind is full of a dozen interests fails to exert the attracting power that is manifested by the man of the one ruling passion, and he fails to draw to him persons, things, and results that will aid in the working out of his plans, and will also fail to place himself in the current of attraction whereby he is brought into contact with those who will be glad to help him because of harmonious interests.

So don't get into the habit of permitting these mental leaks. Keep your Desire fresh and active, and let it get in its work without interference from conflicting desires. Keep in love with the thing you wish to attain - feed your fancy with it - see it as accomplished already, but don't lose your interest. Keep your eye on the main chance, and keep your one ruling passion strong and vigorous. Don't be a mental polygamist - one mental love is all that a man needs - that is, one at a time.

As Ye Sow, So Shall Ye Reap

How does it work? Why do we become what we think about? How it works, as far as we know, can be illuminated by the following analogy that parallels the human mind. Suppose a farmer has some land and it's good, fertile land. Now the land gives the farmer a choice. He may plant in that land whatever he chooses; the land doesn't care. It's up to the farmer to make the decision. Now remember we're comparing the human mind with the land. Because the mind, like the land, doesn't care what you plant in it. It will return what you plant, but it doesn't care what you plant.

Now let's say that the farmer has 2 seeds in his hand. One is a seed of corn, the other is nightshade - a deadly poison. He digs two little holes in the earth and he plants both seeds: one corn, the other nightshade. He covers up the holes, waters and takes care of the land, and what will happen?

Invariably, the land will return what is planted. As is written: "As you sow, so shall you reap". Remember, the land doesn't care. It will return poison in just as wonderful abundance as it will corn. So up come the two plants – one corn, one poison.

Now the human mind is far more fertile, far more incredible and mysterious than the land, but it works the same way. It doesn't care what we plant – success or failure; a concrete, worthwhile goal, or confusion, misunderstanding, fear, anxiety and so on. But what we plant, it will return to us.

You see the human mind is the last, great, unexplored continent on the earth. It contains riches beyond our wildest dreams. It will return anything we want to plant. Now you might say: "Well if that's true, why don't people use their minds more?" Well, there is an answer for that, too.

Our mind comes as standard equipment at birth. It's free, and things that are given to us for nothing we place little value on. Things that we pay money for – we value. The paradox is that exactly the reverse is true: Everything that's really worthwhile in life came to us free – our mind, our soul, our body, our hopes, our dreams, our ambitions, our intelligence, our love of family and children and friends. All these priceless possessions are free, but the things that cost us money are actually very cheap and can be replaced at any time.

A good man can be completely wiped out and make another fortune. He can do that several times. Even if our home burns down, we can rebuild it, but the things we got for nothing we can never replace.

The human mind isn't used merely because we take it for granted.

Familiarity breeds contempt. The mind can do any kind of job we assign to it but generally speaking, we use it for little jobs instead of big, important ones. Universities have proved that most of us are operating on about 10% of our ability.

Decide now: What is it YOU want? Plant your goal in your mind. It's the most important decision you'll ever make in your entire life. You want to be an outstanding salesman, a better worker at your particular job; you want to go places in your company, in your community? All you've got to do is plant that seed in your mind; care for it, work steadily toward your goal – and it will become a reality. It not only will... There's no way that it cannot.

You see, that is the law, like the laws of Sir Isaac Newton, the laws of gravity. If you get on top of a building and jump off, you'll always go down, you'll never go up. And it's the same with all the other laws of nature. They always work; they're inflexible.

Think about your goal in a relaxed, positive way. Picture yourself in your mind's eye as having already achieved this goal. See yourself doing the things you will be doing when you've reached your goal.

Ours have been called the Phenobarbital age, the age of ulcers and nervous breakdowns. At a time when medical research has raised us to a new plateau of good health and longevity, far too many of us worry ourselves into an early grave trying to cope with things in our own, little personal ways, without learning a few great laws that will take care of everything for us.

These things we bring on ourselves to our habitual way of thinking. Every one of us is the sum total of his own thoughts. Each of us must live off the fruit of his thoughts and the future, because what you think today and tomorrow, next month and next year, will mold your life and determine your future. You're guided by your mind.

Mental Healings in the Bible

Down through the ages, men of all nations have somehow instinctively believed that somewhere there resided a healing power which could restore to normal the functions and sensations of man's body. They believed that this strange power could be invoked under certain conditions, and that the alleviation of human suffering would follow. The history of all nations presents testimony in support of this belief.

In the early history of the world the power of secretly influencing men for good or evil, including the healing of the sick, was said to be possessed by the priests and holy men of all nations. Healing of the sick was supposed to be a power derived directly by them from God, and the procedures and processes of healing varied throughout the world. The healing processes took the form of supplications to God attended by various ceremonies, such as the laying on of hands, incantations, application of amulets, talismans, rings, relics, and images.

For example, in the religions of antiquity, priests in the ancient temples gave drugs to the patient and practiced hypnotic suggestions prior to the patient's sleep, telling him that the gods would visit him in his sleep and heal him. Many healings followed. Obviously, all this was the work of potent suggestions to the subconscious mind. In all these healings, the subconscious mind of the subject was the healer.

Throughout the ages, unofficial healers have obtained remarkable results in cases where authorized medical skill has failed. This gives cause for thought. How do these healers in all parts of the world effect their cures? The answer is the blind belief of the sick person, which releases the healing power resident in his subconscious mind.

Many of the remedies and methods employed were rather strange and fantastic, firing the imagination of the patients, and causing an aroused emotional state. This state of mind facilitated the suggestion of health, and was accepted both by the conscious and subconscious mind of the sick.

Biblical Account of the Use of Subconscious Power

What things soever ye desire, when ye pray believe that ye receive them, and ye shall have them.

Note the difference in tenses. The inspired writer tells us to believe and accept as true the fact that our desire has already been accomplished and fulfilled, and that its realization will follow as a thing in the future.

The success of this technique depends on the confident conviction that the thought, the idea, the picture is already a fact in mind. In order for anything to have substance in the realm of mind, it must be thought of as actually existing there.

Here, in a few cryptic words, is a concise and specific direction for making use of the creative power of thought by impressing upon the subconscious the particular thing you desire. Your thought, idea, plan, or purpose is as real on its own plane as your hand or your heart. In following the Biblical technique, you completely eliminate from your mind all consideration of conditions, circumstances, or anything, which might imply adverse contingencies. You are planting a seed (concept) in the mind, which, if you leave it undisturbed, will infallibly germinate into external fruition.

The prime condition is faith. Faith is, in a sense, accepting as true what your reason and senses deny, i.e., a shutting out of the little, rational, analytical, conscious mind and embracing an attitude of complete reliance on the inner power of your subconscious mind.

As you read over and over again in the Bible:

According to your faith is it done unto you...

Permission

I (Ben David) acknowledge BN Publishing for granting me permission to recite printed material from the following books:

The Wisdom of Wallace D. Wattles I - Including: The Science of Getting Rich, The Science of Being Great & The Science of Being Well by Wallace D. Wattles

Thought Vibration or the Law of Attraction in the Thought World & Your Invisible Power (2 Books in 1) by William Walker Atkinson and Genevieve Behrend

Automatic Wealth I: The Secrets of the Millionaire Mind - Including: As a Man Thinketh, the Science of Getting Rich, the

Way to Wealth & Think and Grow Rich by Napoleon Hill, James Allen, Wallace D. Wattles, and Benjamin Franklin

Automatic Wealth III: The Attractor Factor - Including: The Power of Your Subconscious Mind, How to Attract Money by Joseph Murphy, The Law of Attraction AND Feeling Is The Secret

The Dynamic Laws of Prosperity AND Giving Makes You Rich - Special Edition by Catherine Ponder

The Interlinear Bible: Hebrew/English-- The Book of Genesis, with the King James Version (KJV) by King James Version

Torah: The Five Books of Moses - The Interlinear Bible: Hebrew / English

The Psalms: Hebrew Text & English Translation - Parallel Bible: Hebrew/English by JPS

The Richest Man Who Ever Lived: King Solomon's Secrets to Success, Wealth, and Happiness - Vol. 1: The Book Mishle - Proverbs - Hebrew / English by King Solomon and J. P. S.

We have Book Recommendations for you

The Strangest Secret by Earl Nightingale (Audio CD - Jan 2006)

Acres of Diamonds [MP3 AUDIO] [UNABRIDGED] (Audio CD) by Russell H. Conwell

Automatic Wealth: The Secrets of the Millionaire Mind--Including: Acres of Diamonds, As a Man Thinketh, I Dare you!, The Science of Getting Rich, The Way to Wealth, and Think and Grow Rich [UNABRIDGED] by Napoleon Hill, et al (CD-ROM)

Think and Grow Rich [MP3 AUDIO] [UNABRIDGED] by Napoleon Hill, Jason McCoy (Narrator) (Audio CD - January 30, 2006)

As a Man Thinketh [UNABRIDGED]
by James Allen, Jason McCoy (Narrator)
(Audio CD)

Your Invisible Power: How to Attain Your
Desires by Letting Your Subconscious
Mind Work for You [MP3 AUDIO]
[UNABRIDGED]
by Genevieve Behrend, Jason McCoy
(Narrator) (Audio CD)

Thought Vibration or the Law of Attraction
in the Thought World [MP3 AUDIO]
[UNABRIDGED]
by William Walker Atkinson, Jason McCoy
(Narrator) (Audio CD - July 1, 2005)

The Law of Success Volume I: The
Principles of Self-Mastery by Napoleon
Hill (Audio CD - Feb 21, 2006)

The Law of Success, Volume I: The
Principles of Self-Mastery (Law of Success,
Vol 1) (The Law of Success) by Napoleon
Hill (Paperback - Jun 20, 2006)

**The Law of Success , Volume II & III: A
Definite Chief Aim & Self Confidence by
Napoleon Hill (Paperback - Jun 20, 2006)**

**Thought Vibration or the Law of Attraction
in the Thought World & Your Invisible
Power (Paperback)**

Automatic Wealth, The Secrets of the Millionaire Mind-Including:As a Man Thinketh, The Science of Getting Rich, The Way to Wealth and Think and Grow Rich (Paperback)

The Bestsellers on this Book give sound advice about money or how to obtain it. Just shoot to the stars and stay focused on your dreams and it will happen. There is nothing that we can imagine, that we can't do. So what are we waiting for, let's begin the journey of self fullfillment.

4 Bestsellers in 1 Book:

As a Man Thinketh by James Allen

The Science of Getting Rich by Wallace D. Wattles

The Way to Wealth by Benjamin Franklin

Think and Grow Rich by Napoleon Hill

BN Publishing

Improving People's Life

www.bnpublishing.com

BN Publishing

Improving People's Life

www.bnpublishing.com

BN Publishing

Improving People's Life

www.bnpublishing.com

BN Publishing

Improving People's Life

www.bnpublishing.com

BN Publishing

Improving People's Life

www.bnpublishing.com

Printed in the United States
81374LV00001B/31-33

9 789562 914024